101 THINGS
NOT TO SAY
DURING SEX

101 THINGS NOT TO SAY DURING SEX

Patti Putnicki
Illustrations by Dusty Rumsey

WARNER BOOKS

A Time Warner Company

•

Copyright © 1993 by JSA Publications, Inc.

All rights reserved.

Warner Books, Inc., 1271 Avenue of the Americas, New York, NY 10020

 A Time Warner Company

Printed in the United States of America

First Printing: October 1993

10 9 8 7 6 5 4 3 2 1

LIBRARY OF CONGRESS CATALOGING — IN — PUBLICATION DATA

Putnicki, Patti.
    101 things not to say during sex / Patti Putnicki.
        p.   cm.
    ISBN 0-446-39511-0
    1. Sex—Humor.   2. Sex–Caricatures and cartoons.   I. Title.
    II. Title: One hundred one things not to say during sex.
    III. Title: One hundred and one things not to say during sex.
    PN6231 . S54P87 1993
    818'.5402—dc20   93-8298
                                                                       CIP

Cover Illustration by Dusty Rumsey

Patti and Dusty wish to thank the following individuals for their support and encouragement:

Joseph S. Ajlouny, our agent; Mauro DiPreta, our editor;
Brian Healy, our production coordinator;
Jerry Jenkins and Jeff Soper, our mentors;
and to Gwen, Elena, Jan, Bryan, Cheryl, Gary, Robert and Donna,
who taught us "not to say" so much.
We also wish to thank all the folks who have never said any of
the things we've described herein. You are a credit to your race
even if you are too polite to be any fun at all.

101 THINGS NOT TO SAY DURING SEX

1

2

3

4

5

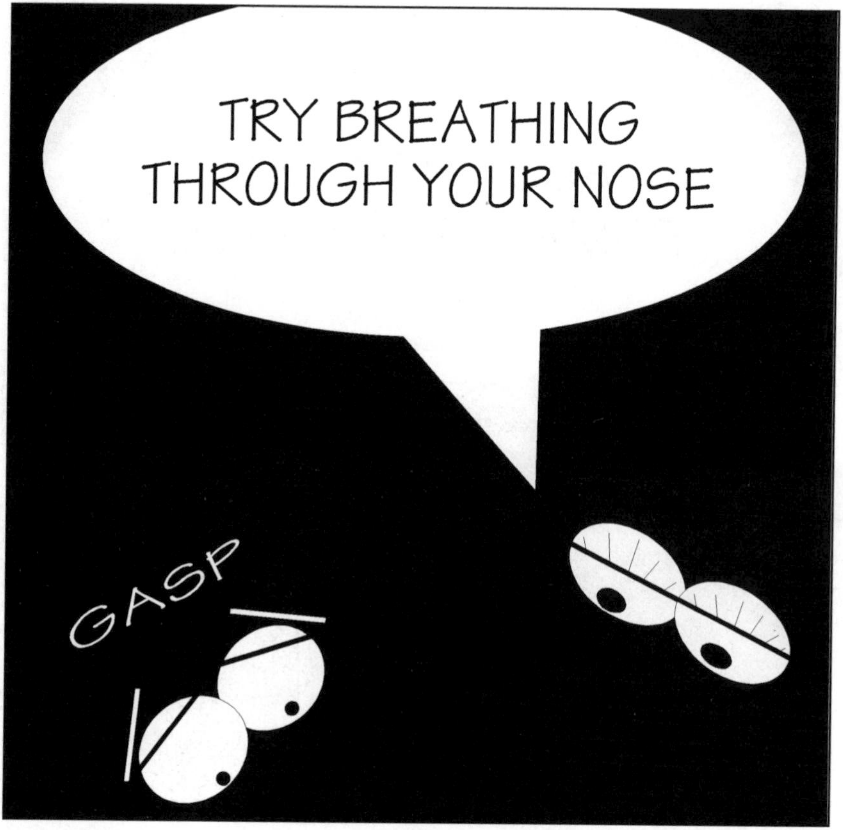
TRY BREATHING THROUGH YOUR NOSE
GASP

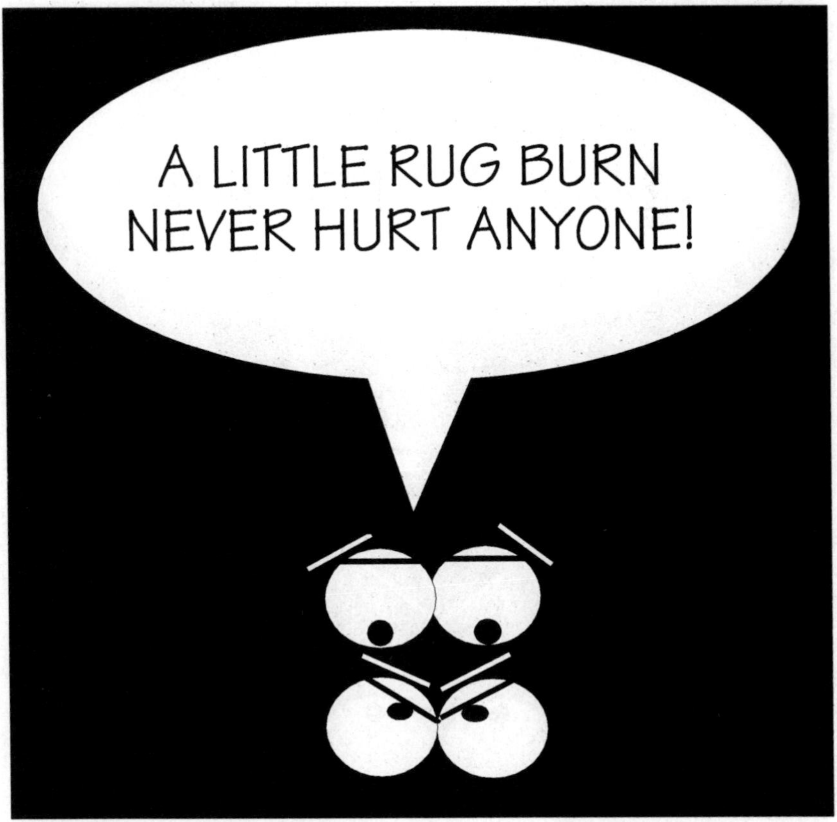
A LITTLE RUG BURN
NEVER HURT ANYONE!

8

9

11

12

13

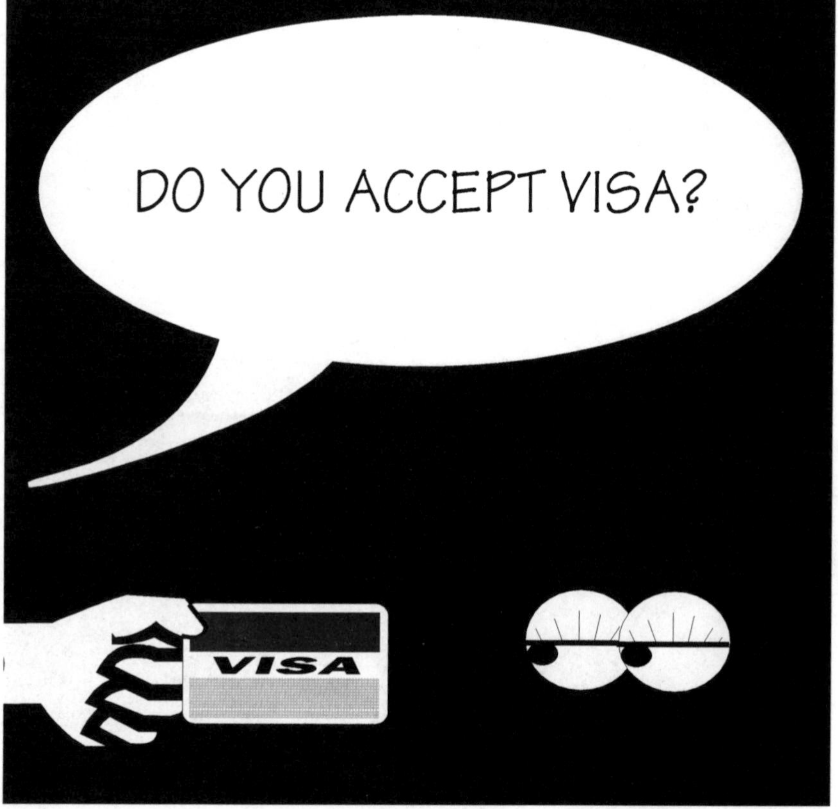
DO YOU ACCEPT VISA?
VISA

16

17

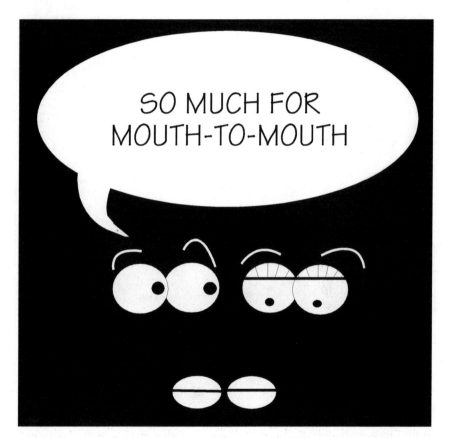

18

19

23

24

28

31

33

34

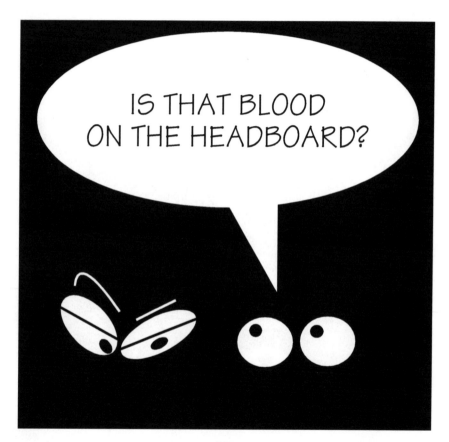

39

40

41

43

45

47

48

50

51

54

56

59

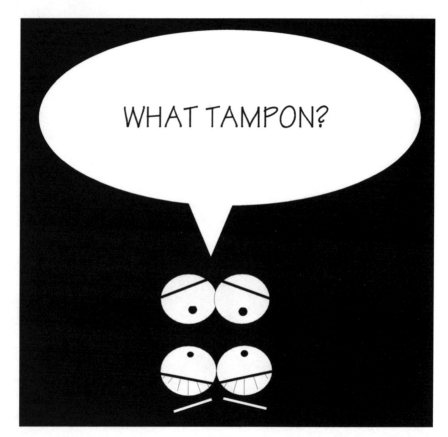

61

64

68

69

71

72

73

75

78

81

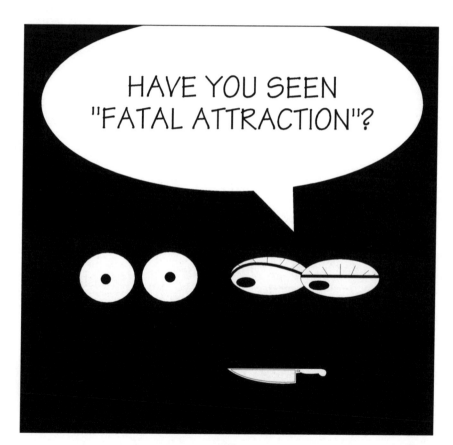

82

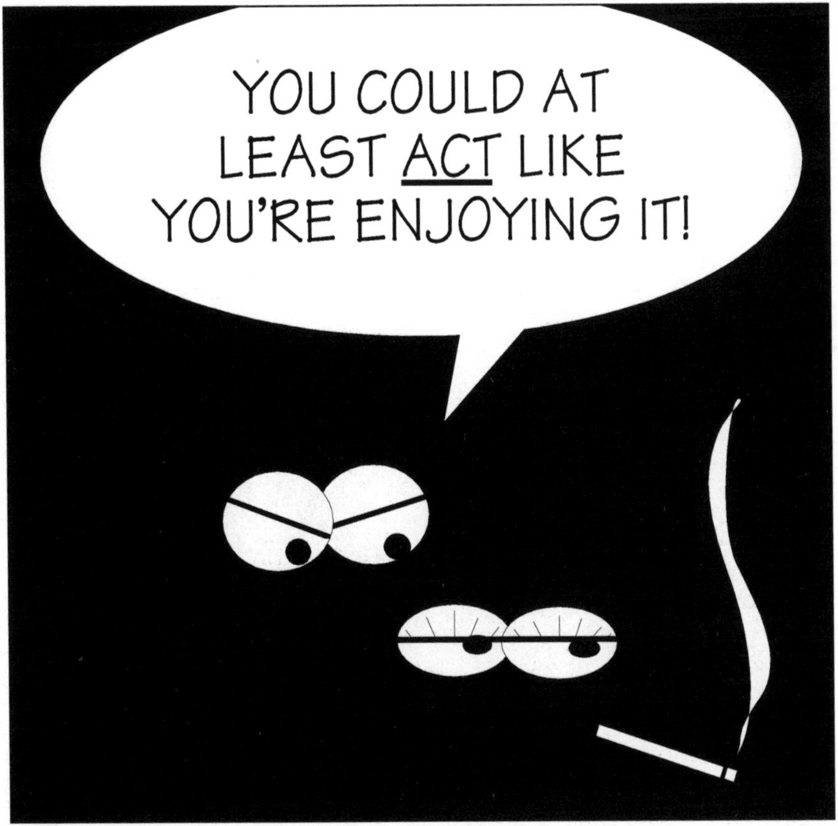
YOU COULD AT LEAST ACT LIKE YOU'RE ENJOYING IT!

95

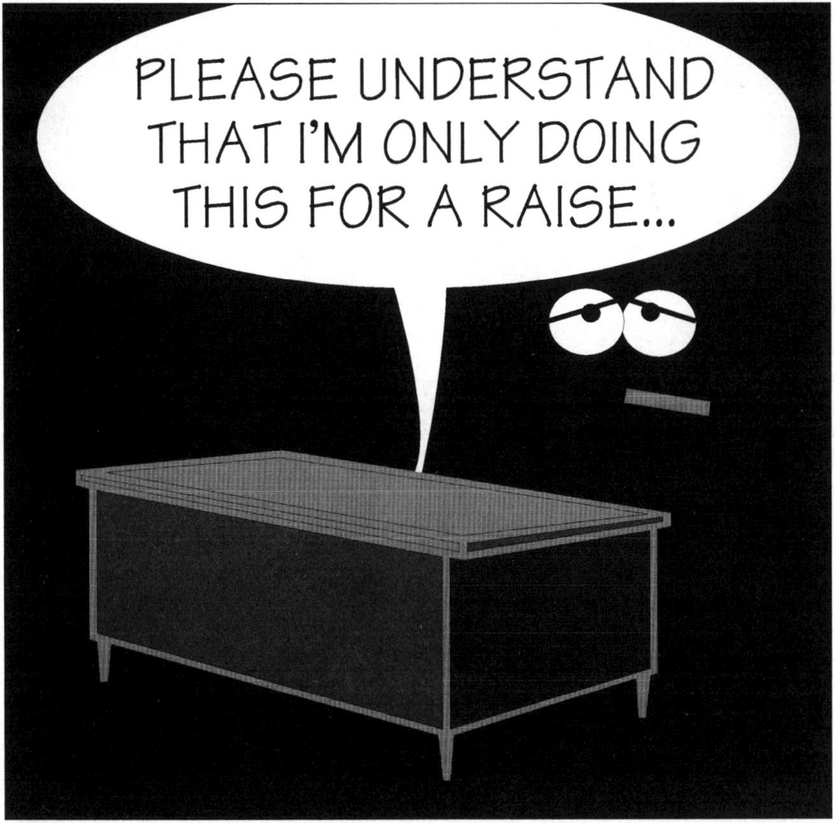
PLEASE UNDERSTAND THAT I'M ONLY DOING THIS FOR A RAISE...

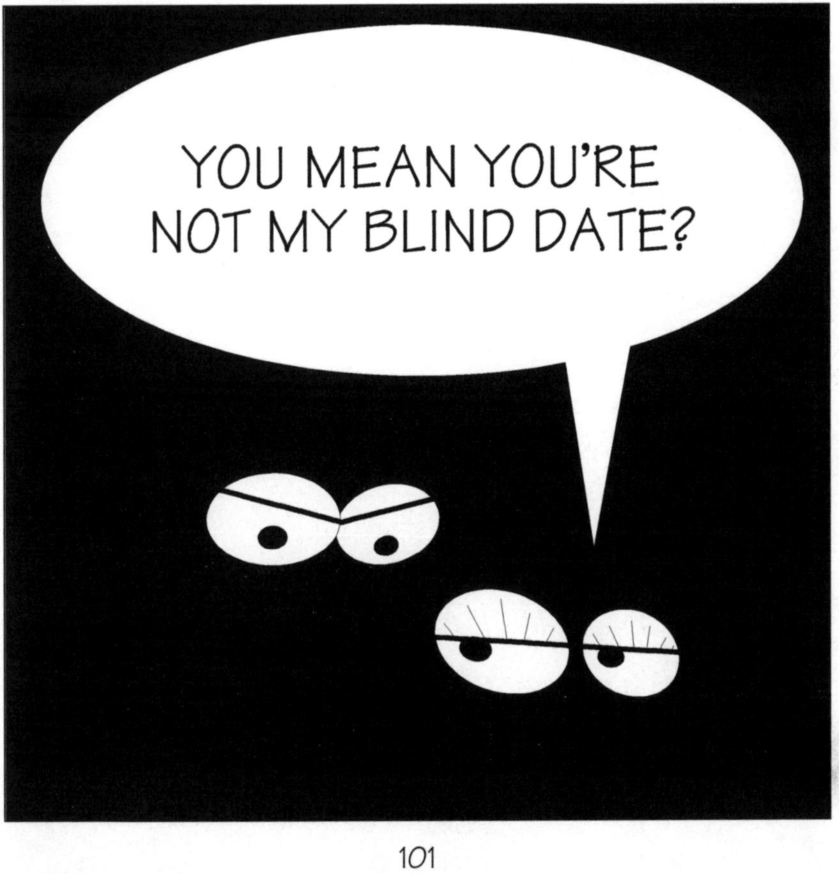
YOU MEAN YOU'RE
NOT MY BLIND DATE?